PERSONAL SCRUM

Simon Kneafsey

Contents

CHAPTER ONE
Introduction

Origins Of The Personal Scrum System

The Personal Scrum System is simple, and it works! It can help you achieve your Goals, whatever they might be. The effort will come from you, but the system will help ensure you direct your efforts correctly and maintain focus over the long term. Big Goals take time to achieve, and the Personal Scrum system will allow you to work towards them in small and meaningful steps.

Some people drift through life without direction or Goals. They are directed by the forces and people around them. Some people are happy like this. Others are not. This book is for those that are not, those who want to take control of their lives and achieve something that requires dedication and effort. Personal Scrum will enable you to use a set of tried and tested practices to help you achieve success.

To do this, you will need to decide what you want to achieve, set Goals, and then work towards them. Doing this will ensure you move forward in life with intent, and the Personal Scrum System is designed to help you accomplish this.

It has helped me do this throughout the ten years I have used it. During this time, I set and achieved the following Goals:

- Become a leading authority on Scrum as a Professional Scrum Trainer with Scrum.org.

- Built a successful global training business - TheScrumMaster.co.uk.
- Conducted training courses for Google, NASA, The United Nations, Coca-Cola, Toyota, and many more.
- Taught 10,000+ people about Scrum.
- Grown TheScrumMaster.co.uk by partnering with Associate Trainers all over the world.
- Created resources used by hundreds of thousands of people to learn about Scrum.
- Written and published this book, with more to come.

The Personal Scrum System is based on the Scrum framework created by Ken Schwaber and Jeff Sutherland. Although inspired by Scrum, the Personal Scrum System is not the same and is intended for a different purpose. It is further influenced by concepts and practices from Agile, Lean & Kanban.

A big thank you to Ken & Jeff. Their work has changed the world for the better and helped millions of people in so many ways. They should be household names like Steve Jobs and Bill Gates!

Scrum helps teams to do complex work, such as building software. The Personal Scrum System helps individuals succeed in another complex domain - their lives. Life is complex and unpredictable, and we all have to deal with it daily. The Personal Scrum System helps people find success in their lives by setting and achieving Goals.

About Simon Kneafsey

I spent the early part of my career as a Software Developer working for large consultancies and Media companies. Around 2005, I came across Scrum, and everything changed. The first few products I helped build using Scrum were successful, and I knew I had discovered something special that could also help others.

I then spent years helping a range of organisations adopt Scrum. I made many mistakes and learnt a lot along the way. As part of one role, I had to train people about Scrum and realised how much I loved teaching and training. I decided that this is what I wanted to do for the next part of my life.

Shortly after Ken Schwaber started Scrum.org, I recognised that becoming a Scrum.org Professional Scrum Trainer (PST) would allow me to teach more people about Scrum. I achieved this Goal in 2012, but I only did a little training in the first few years. I realised that being a PST was not enough and that I needed to learn how to build a training business around this capability.

In 2015, I launched my training company - TheScrumMaster.co.uk. Since then, I have travelled the world teaching people about Scrum and have helped 10,000+ people in 35+ countries. As demand continued to grow, I added a group of Associate Trainers and a customer support team so we could service the demand from our clients. I also formalised the mission of TheScrumMaster.co.uk, which is to help 1 million people to learn about Scrum. To support this ambitious Goal, I created a range of new digital products, including Practice Assessments & Video Courses, which have been used by over 250,000 people since.

My most recent Goal was to write this book. I also always wanted to write a book, and this seemed like the perfect time. If it goes well, I may even write some more. I wanted to share the Personal Scrum System I have created, the same system that has helped me achieve my own Goals. Anyone who is willing can benefit from this as much as I have.

All this was made possible by the Personal Scrum System. This was the system I created and used to set my Goals, plan my Activities, and stay focused as I made small, incremental progress. I realised that beyond all the other things I have learned and taught over the years, the Personal Scrum System has the most potential to help other people. Writing this book was a way for me to share this with a broader audience. I hope you will learn about it and use it, and I am sure it will help you as it helped me.

About Scrum

Scrum is a lightweight framework that helps people create value when doing complex work. It helps people develop products where there is a high level of uncertainty and change. Scrum in a nutshell:

- A Product Owner orders the work for a complex problem into a Product Backlog.
- The Scrum Team turns a selection of the work into an Increment of Value during a Sprint.
- The Scrum Team and its stakeholders inspect the results and adjust the plan & process for the next Sprint.
- Repeat.

Scrum is simple to learn and use. It helps people to work iteratively and incrementally using an empirical approach. Empiricism encourages increased Transparency, Inspection, and Adaptation. It exposes issues and real progress as early as possible and encourages people to make changes to increase their chances of success.

Ken Schwaber and Jeff Sutherland created Scrum in the 1990s. Scrum was initially used to build software, but is now used by tens of millions of people worldwide to help solve complex challenges, and this number is growing rapidly. You can read the Scrum Guide for the official definition of Scrum.

I have been working with Scrum for over 15 years and have helped hundreds of organisations and thousands of people to use it to improve their ability to deliver value. I have seen people build incredible products and help their organisations to improve. I have realised that although Scrum was designed to help teams, it can also help individuals.

Around ten years ago, I began to use a variation of Scrum to organise my life. To set Goals, create plans, and then manage the Activities required to reach them. It seemed logical to use Scrum as I was spending so much time talking about it and helping others to learn about it.

Before this, I had set the occasional Goal and used To Do lists to manage my work. Whilst I had achieved some things this way, I realise, looking back now, that I lacked focus, and the one-dimensional nature of To Do lists was limiting my ability to tackle more nuanced tasks.

Everything changed once I started to use Scrum to organise myself. Each year I achieved massive amounts and made real progress toward my goals. We often overestimate what we can accomplish in a week and underestimate what we can achieve in a year. By monitoring and tracking my progress, I started to see just what was possible, and everything changed for me.

In a few short years, I became a leading authority on Scrum and built a successful training business. I have realised that perhaps the most significant potential for Scrum in the future is to help individuals as it helped me. What I developed from the Scrum framework I have called the Personal Scrum System, and this book is my effort to share with others what worked for me. The guidance it contains has been tried and tested over many years. Whilst it is an adaption of Scrum, it is still based on the Scrum framework, and much remains the same.

About The Personal Scrum System

The Personal Scrum System is founded on Empiricism. Empiricism states that knowledge is based on experience. It emphasises the use of experiments and is the basis of the scientific method that has led to the human race's most significant advances that have changed the world.

Life is complex, but taking an empirical approach to your life can give you "superpowers". By practising an empirical approach, you will increase the transparency of your current situation. Regular inspection of what is happening in your environment and frequently adapting to things will help you improve your life in the manner you truly desire, and the best method to do this is using the Personal Scrum System. It will help you determine, set, and achieve Goals, whatever your Goals may be.

Many people do not take the time to stop and think about what they want, what success would look like for them, and what Goals they need to set and achieve to get that success. This is a mistake. If you drift through life without Goals and a strategy to reach them, it is far less likely that you will get what you want. You will more likely be at the mercy of others and will spend your time helping them achieve their Goals and helping them become successful.

The Personal Scrum System will change that. It requires that you decide what success looks like for you, set your Goals, and then start working towards them. Your definition of success and Goals may change, but the critical thing is to have some Goals and start progressively working towards them.

CHAPTER TWO
Success

What Is Success?

The purpose of the Personal Scrum System is to help you achieve your Goals and be successful. But what is success?

The short answer is that success means different things to all of us. We are all influenced by the culture that surrounds us, so success often includes some of the following:

- Having a good job
- Achieving fame
- Gaining money and wealth
- Being healthy
- Supporting a family

Many of us will value some or all of these things, but at some point in our lives, we may realise they are not enough. We may re-evaluate and change our view of success. Here are some alternative views of success:

- Starting and building a business.
- Moving forward and being open to self-growth.
- Having quality relationships and being able to spend time with people you love.
- A sense of giving back to the world and making a difference
- Mastering something.

* * *

We each need to define what success looks like for us. It is OK not to know the answer or for our definition to change over time. But we should not ignore the question. If you do not know what success looks like for you, then you will not be able to work towards achieving it. And if you don't even know what success is, you will probably never achieve it.

Success != Happiness

"What is the ultimate quantification of success? For me, it's not how much time you spend doing what you love. It's how little time you spend doing what you hate." - Casey Neistat.

For many people, the definition of success is to be happy. But happiness isn't a Goal you can reach and be done with. It is a constant pursuit that requires continual re-evaluation and Activity. The Hedonic Treadmill[1] is the observed tendency of humans to quickly return to a relatively stable level of happiness despite major positive or adverse events. According to this theory, as a person achieves more success, expectations and desires rise in parallel, resulting in no permanent happiness gain.

Pursuing a Goal (which will likely include your current definition of happiness and success) and regularly setting and reviewing your Goals is vital. What makes you successful and happy today may not be the same as tomorrow. Failure to recognise this and adapt may result in failure and unhappiness.

CHAPTER THREE
Goals

Why Set Goals?

Setting clear and measurable Goals and working towards them each week is the basis of the Personal Scrum System. Successful people set Goals. People who set Goals will often write them down and work toward them. If you do not set Goals, you are adrift, and external forces and other people will direct your work. Those people will not have your best interests at heart. Their Goals will become your Goals.

When I started working as a Junior Software Developer for a large Consultancy in the late 1990s, I had no clear Goals for a long time. My only Goal for my first year at work was to survive in the role and not get fired.

Over time, I observed that the most respected people in the company were the technical experts. Management relied on them to solve complex problems, design solutions, and plan and price work. They were invited to important meetings, and the clients always requested them by name when commissioning their projects. Undoubtedly, they were also contracted for huge daily rates and paid very well as a result. As a Junior Software Developer who understood little about anything, this looked attractive to me. I wanted to be like the technical experts but did not know how to get there.

The only Strategic Goal I had at this point was a vague idea in the back of my mind to become a technical expert like the ones I saw and envied. The only intermediate Goals I had were also only in my mind. They were to pick up as much knowledge as possible as fast as possible. I planned to request as much training as my boss would allow so I could learn more about anything that might turn out to be helpful.

I doubt I even voiced my vague Goal to my boss when I had performance reviews. My boss did occasionally send me to get training, but this was only when the training was for a skill required on the current project.

As a result, I worked hard and learnt a lot, but never really picked up deep expertise in anything. Because I was naturally a team player with a desire to please and be helpful, I became a Utility Developer, someone with a broad range of experience in many things, but no deep expertise in anything. This was what the company needed but not what I wanted. Because my Goals were vague, I didn't work towards them and instead followed the path someone laid out for me. Eventually, I realised I was unsatisfied with my work and left the organisation, looking for a new challenge elsewhere.

Without a Goal and a sense of progress, there is no point in our work. You keep working week after week, month after month, year after year, and you don't move in the direction you want. For most people, this becomes deeply unsatisfying. Every journey needs to have a destination. Your Goals are your destinations. Your plan is your path. Your measures help you check that you are moving down that path.

If you want to achieve something, no matter how big, unique or challenging it may be, it is essential that you define your long-term strategic Goal and then set smaller intermediate Goals to help you reach and achieve that strategic Goal.

You can do a lot in a year if you plan and focus, or achieve little if you have no direction and only focus on the urgent things right in front of you. You may not reach all the Goals by the end of the year, but you will make progress and be moving in the right direction.

What If I Don't Know What My Goal Should Be?

"There are only two human problems: (1) knowing what you want, but not knowing how to get it; and (2) not knowing what you want." - Stephen Covey,

The 7 Habits of Highly Effective People[1].

Some people fail to set Goals and work toward them as they are unsure of what they want to do. They believe that they will figure out what they want to do in the future, and then they can set the Goal and start working towards it. I can tell you from experience that this is not the right approach.

You should always have a Goal and work towards it, even if you are unsure if it is the right Goal. Once you get used to this approach, it is easy to set a new Goal and change direction when you discover something new that you want to achieve. It is much easier to change direction when moving forward than to start moving in the first place.

"A body at rest tends to stay at rest" - The second

law of thermodynamics[2].

Starting is hard, so start now and keep moving while you work out the right Goals and direction. When you are progressing, you are more likely to spot opportunities that help you figure out the right Goal.

For many years I thought I wanted to be a Senior Software Developer, then a Project Manager, then a Development Manager, and then a Scrum Master. Some Goals were good for a time; others were bad for me from the start. What they all did was help me figure out what I wanted to do.

I hated being a Project Manager, but that helped me realise I wanted to become a Scrum Master. Initially I enjoyed and revelled in being a Scrum Master, but eventually I burned out trying to help organisations move into the 21st century. This led me to do some teaching and discover what I truly enjoyed. Teaching would energise rather than burn me out. From there, I became a Professional Scrum Trainer with Scrum.org & TheScrumMaster.co.uk.

Your current Goal is still just a step. The next step for me is to be an author, and then I will see where it takes me next. If I don't know the Goal after the current Goal, I will figure it out as I work towards reaching the first Goal.

When I set myself the Goal of becoming a Scrum.org Professional Scrum Trainer I knew there was a long path to follow and much work required. I also knew that most people that started towards this Goal were not able to achieve it. So, the day I was told I had made it, I was both elated and had a true sense of accomplishment, my hard work and dedication had paid off.

However, I soon realised this was a new start, not the end. Being qualified to train did not mean I could train. When I struggled to fill courses, I realised another Goal I needed to set and work towards: learning the business of training. Only then could I fill and run classes and be a Trainer in action rather than just in name.

Setting Good Goals

Most of the Activities you do should be directed towards helping you achieve your Goals. Some of the Goals you have and work on will be facilitating other people's Goals, especially if you are an employee. You will be paid to work to achieve someone else's Goals. That is the nature of being employed. Hopefully, you have a job where those Goals will become your Goals, and you will benefit from working towards them in ways that exceed the immediate financial reward.

In my early career as a Software Developer, I was employed to write code that solved problems for other people. I did this primarily to earn a monthly salary to pay my bills, but I quickly realised an additional benefit of this work linked to my Goals. By being paid to write code, I was given the opportunity to learn how to code. In the future, this skill could be used to my advantage.

Not all your activities will be linked to a Goal, which is also fine. In life, there are many things that we have to do. Some stuff must be done to live and be part of society. Examples of this type of Activity are paying bills, filing a tax return, shopping and commuting.

Be careful that you don't get stuck only doing this necessary but low-value stuff. Don't only prioritise these essential but relatively unimportant Activities. When we are short of time and lack Goals, it is easy to focus only on these low-value but essential Activities. Months and years will pass, and you will find yourself no further forward in your life and will not have achieved any Goals. This stuff is an essential distraction but should not become your focus.

Find ways to minimise the time and effort around the essential but not Goal related Activities. Working towards Goals and becoming successful will require you to change how you structure your life and do things differently to other people. To minimise the time I spend doing essential but low-value Activities, I now do the following:

- Shop online exclusively and have everything delivered.
- Eliminate commuting by working from home to save commuting time.
- Only conduct face-to-face meetings when it is essential to reduce travel time. I carry out 95+% of my meetings online and I have done for 10+ years. It is even easier now as most people have also caught on to this trend.
- Set default meeting times for 30 mins rather than 1 hour, which is more than enough in most cases.

When some new need appears, our instinct is to act on it straight away. Newness often makes something more attractive than anything else. But beware! You should always stop to ask if this has to be done now. Whenever possible, add it to your To Do List and return to evaluate it later. Many things that seem like a good idea in the moment turn out to be less critical when reconsidered later. This is one reason why Weekly Planning is so important. You can add new work to a list and revisit it later as part of Weekly Planning. This simple approach helps you stay focussed on what you had originally planned and better prioritise or even eliminate low-value Activities.

Wherever possible, aim to question and, if possible, eliminate non-Goal related Activities. An Activity may be essential and valuable, but is it Goal orientated? If not, should you be doing it? Some things have to be done, but sometimes this is not the case, and it doesn't help you move towards your Goal. Do you really need to do it? Ideas and sources of Activity are unlimited. Your time and energy are limited, so identifying the things NOT to do is a critical skill to develop. If you can't bear to lose it, add it to the Ideas List for later. I find this a good practice, and I rarely work on the things that have sat on my Ideas List for any time. If they are good ideas, you will keep returning to them and promote them to the To Do List. They may even spawn new Goals.

These approaches are all vital as it is easy to get side-tracked with seemingly important stuff that simply distracts us from achieving our Goals. We need the discipline to stay focused. Some people lack this and don't work to develop it, so they spend their whole life directionless and often unsatisfied. If you don't set and work towards your Goals, you will spend your life working on someone else's Goals!

Here are some of the characteristics of effective Goals:

- Written - If you haven't written it down, you won't be clear or focused on it. It won't seem real or tangible, and you are unlikely to be highly motivated to work towards it.
- Committed - For a Goal to be motivating, it must give meaning to an action that will follow. If you don't commit to the Goal, you won't achieve it.
- Specific - Specific Goals are preferable. Setting the right measure around a Goal increases the likelihood of achieving it. More on this later.
- Challenging - Goals should be challenging enough to be attainable but not so challenging that they seem impossible.
- Feedback - Many people benefit from working with others to achieve Goals. Even if you go it alone, getting feedback and encouragement from others can be a big motivator. When Goals are completed, it's time to celebrate with others!

What Type Of Goals

What type of Goals should you set? The answer depends on your interests, aspirations for your life, where you are currently and what is most important to you. The Goals you create and focus on will be unique to you.

I have found that I tend to set Goals in each of the following areas:

- Health & Happiness
- Work & Business
- Family & Friends
- Investments
- Personal Development

In any given year, I will have Goals under each category, and the balance has changed over time. When I started formally setting and tracking my Goals, most of them were in the Work & Business category. Many years later, although my work is still massively important to me, more of my Goals fall into the other categories, and I am aiming for more of a balance between them. In particular, I am focussing more on Health & Happiness, which I realise is increasingly important as I get older.

Establishing your Goals should not be too hard. Take some time alone, eliminate distractions and think about what you want to achieve and where you want to get to in the future.

What is important to you? What do you want to be remembered for? What do you want to be successful at? What do you enjoy doing? What do you care deeply about? These questions and more can help you reflect on what matters to you and set Goals that will help you get more of it, whatever your "it" is.

As you spend more time thinking about your Goals and working towards them, you will discover more about what you want, which may lead you to change your Goals. This is normal when you first start doing all of this. If you realise a Goal is no longer essential to you, or you consistently neglect to act on that Goal, then it is likely an indicator to change the Goal. We all have limited time, so focussing on the right Goals is essential. If your Goals are not suitable for you now, change them.

Another challenge people face when focusing on Goals is deciding how many Goals to set. This depends on many factors, and the final number will be unique to you.

- Are you employed or self-employed? If you are employed, then a significant portion of your time and the Goals associated with it will belong to someone else. There is nothing wrong with this. To be successful in your job, you should still identify and track your Goals and can use the Personal Scrum System for this. The more you get done and the more value you create at work, the better you will do and the more benefits you will likely receive.
- Do you have a family that requires significant time? E.g. young children or elderly parents. If you do, then some of your Goals will likely relate to these other important people and so may be more about them than you. That is fine, but you will need to recognise this and account for the time this will take, meaning you will have less available for Goals specific to you.
- Do you have significant existing other commitments? This could be your weekly Golf game, volunteering

work or attendance at a club. If you do, then it is likely you already have Goals in these areas and are working towards them even if you have not stopped to write them down. You should reflect on them and ensure you are happy with the commitments and Goals you already have.

Reaching Your Goals

Reaching Goals almost always takes longer than we expect. Most people overestimate what they can achieve in a day but underestimate what they can achieve in a year. Many small steps in the right direction start to add up and make a difference over the long run. Once you are on the path, don't underestimate the effort, patience and perseverance required to achieve essential Goals.

When we start down a path towards a Goal that we have inevitably not taken before, many things will happen that we cannot predict. We will be unaware of the many Activities we will need to do. We will likely underestimate how long many things will take. We may forget about sickness, holidays, emergencies, distractions, and unexpected occurrences that all add up to slow us down or divert us. This is all inevitable. Don't give up!

Weekly Planning and Quarterly Planning are essential. They ensure we regularly inspect our Goals and progress towards them and re-plan based on what may have changed or emerged. The regular planning sessions help ensure we maintain focus and re-plan frequently as we progress towards our Goals.

The Power Of Having Clear Goals

Will Smith writes in his memoir "Will" that he studied Tom Cruise's press tours while planning how he would become the biggest film star in the world, a bigger one than even Tom Cruise himself.

Smith had already seen success with his hit sitcom "The Fresh Prince of Bel-Air", but he was eager to make the jump to being a global film star. That's when Smith got some essential advice from Arnold Schwarzenegger. *"You are not a movie star if your movies are only successful in America. You are not a movie star until every person in every country on earth knows who you are. You have to travel the globe, shake every hand, kiss every baby. Think of yourself as a politician running for Biggest Movie Star in the World."*

"I started to notice how much other actors hate traveling, press, and promoting. It seemed like utter insanity to me", Smith writes, admitting that Schwarzenegger's advice made him *"scan the field of my competition to see who else knew, who else held the secret."* Smith's research led him to Cruise, who *"was the head of the pack."*

"I started quietly monitoring all of Tom's global promotional Activities", Smith writes. *"When I arrived in a country to promote my movie, I would ask the local movie executives to give me Tom's promotional schedule. And I vowed to do two hours more than whatever he did in every country."*

"Unfortunately, Tom Cruise is either a cyborg, or there are six of

him" Smith adds. *"I was receiving reports of four-and-a-half-hour stretches on red carpets in Paris, London, Tokyo… In Berlin, Tom literally signed every single autograph until there was no one else who wanted one. Tom Cruise's global promotions were the individual best in Hollywood."*

To beat Cruise, Smith turned to his music career and made sure his international press tours for movies included live performances outside of film premieres to draw thousands of fans. *"Tom couldn't do that — neither could Arnold, Bruce, or Sly,"* the actor writes. *"I'd found my way out of the entertainment news segment and into headline news. And once your movie moves from entertainment to news, it's no longer a movie — it's a cultural phenomenon."*

Here is a summary of Will Smiths goals and the results that followed:

- **Strategic Goal** - Being the biggest movie star in the world.
- **Intermediate Goal 1** - Work harder than Tom Cruise when promoting a film.
- **Failed**. Tom Cruise was the best at this and hard work alone would not be enough to beat him.
- **Intermediate Goal 2** - Make the movie a cultural phenomenon by using music career to draw in and connect with more fans.
- **Success**. Will Smith becomes the biggest movie star in the world. The only actor to have eight consecutive films gross more than $100 million at the US box office and 10 consecutive films gross more than $150 million internationally.[1]

Measuring Progress

Once we have set Goals, it is important to put some measures in place that we can use to understand if we are making progress or have achieved the Goal. If you don't quantify what achieving your Goal will look like, how will you know when you have achieved it? Measuring progress can reveal how close you are to accomplishing a goal. This may remind you of what you're working to achieve and give you the motivation to keep going.

Measuring your progress can also help you understand if the Activities you are focussing on are having an impact and moving you in the right direction. Your measures may indicate the need to adjust your plan to improve the chances of success.

"If you can't measure it, you can't manage it." - Peter Drucker [1]

Aim for simple, easy-to-gather, and motivating measures. Here are some examples of the Goals & Measures I set while writing this book:

- **Goal** - Write 1st draft of Personal Scrum System Book
- **Measure** - Write 1000 words daily at least five days a week.
- **Goal** - Personal Scrum System Book Is Successful.
- **Measures** - Gain at least a 4-star rating and 15 reviews on Amazon.

* * *

As you can see, the Goals & Measures are short, clear, and easy to check. The measures serve an essential purpose of helping me understand if I am successfully achieving my goals.

CHAPTER FOUR

The Personal Scrum System

Visualising Your Goals And Activities

Visualising your Goals and the Activities by writing them down is a critical process. Your brain is like the best supercomputer ever invented. It can hold vast amounts of information and process complex sets of variables to deliver a result. It does vast amounts of work in the background without us even being aware, keeping us safe and dealing with and processing a constant stream of data and stimuli.

Unlike a real computer, the brain has finite resources and starts to slow down and fail when those resources are expended. If we over-exert it, the results it supplies may be suboptimal and cause problems. Our brain needs food, water and sleep to continue performing. Because your brain is so critical, it is essential to look after it and save its vital powers for things you really need it to do.

The brain has both short-term and long-term memory. Short-term memory helps us to process inputs and make good decisions. The more things we try and hold in our short-term memory, the more resources we use and the higher the risk that the brain loses some of its vital data. This cognitive load expends resources we could better use elsewhere, like helping us solve a complex problem or learn something new.

For this reason, it is crucial not to store non-essential information in your short-term memory. Data not being used to solve problems does not need to take up space and resources in your short-term memory.

We are fortunate to live in an age where we all have access to near unlimited amounts of additional storage space to ease the strain on our brains. Computers, phones and the internet mean that we are all closely connected to digital information stores where we can save and retrieve information whenever we need it without using our brains for storage.

Your Goals and Activities should be stored digitally to save space in your short-term memory. Don't use your brain to store stuff that isn't needed to solve a problem or help you make a decision. Make a note of it and free your memory to handle other, more important stuff. A computer is an extension of your brain. Use it. This is another superpower that anyone can access.

Another considerable benefit of storing Goals and Activities outside the brain is that it reduces anxiety. Having to constantly hold onto, order, and analyse the things we need to do ends up becoming something the subconscious deals with constantly in the background. Without us even realising it, this can increase anxiety if the brain struggles to fit things in or process all the changes. This background Activity can make it harder for us to rest and sleep. The less rested we are, the less well the brain will perform. It can become a vicious circle. Free your mind from this content churning by externalising this information, thus allowing your subconscious to let go of it.

I find that at the end of a working day, updating my Daily Plan for the next day releases everything from my mind and frees my brain to move on to something else (or nothing at all). It can get the rest it needs and ensure a good night's sleep, so I am ready for the next day's challenges.

The Personal Scrum System includes 8 Lists that hold your Goals and Activities. These Lists should be captured on a Kanban board. "Kanban" is the Japanese word for visual signal. A Kanban board helps make intangible Goals and Activities easier to manage by making them visible. If you want to manage your Goals and Activities, you need to be able to see them.

Ideas List	Goals List	To Do List	This Week List	Today List	In Progress List	On Hold List	Done List

Personal Scrum Lists Kanban Board Example

Another benefit of externalising your Goals and Activities by writing them down is that it helps make them more real, which is a big step towards making them happen. You are less likely to forget them. You can more easily review them. You can share them with others. You can compare this year's Goals with last year's. You can visualise relationships between Goals and Activities. The advantages are numerous.

You can create a Kanban board anywhere. Some people like to make their Kanban board prominent and visible using tape, index cards and post-it notes. Whilst this does have the significant benefit of making it tangible and visible, it has the limitation of being tied to a physical location where you may or may not be at the time you need to access it.

I prefer to use a digital Kanban board so I can carry it and access it whenever I want. I can also update it at any time, reducing the cognitive load on my short-term memory whenever I want.

Overview Of Personal Scrum

The **Personal Scrum System** is simple but effective. You can learn about it and start to use it in less than an hour. The system defines lists where you make your **Goals** and **Activities** transparent. Making them visible and clearly defined increases the likelihood you will achieve them.

The **Personal Scrum System** separates Goals (where you want to get to), Measures (how you know you are getting there), Activities (what you need to do to reach your Goals) and Tasks (what you need to do to complete the Activities). These distinct groups provide a logical hierarchy that helps you understand how the low-level Tasks you carry out ultimately contribute to your Goals.

First, you define your **Goals**. These can be big or small and in any area of your life where you want to make progress. You add these **Goals** to your **Goals List**. You should assign some **Measures** to your **Goals** to help you understand if you are making meaningful progress towards them over time.

Next, you define the **Activities** you will do to reach these **Goals**. You add these to your **To Do List**.

When you have new ideas for **Goals** and **Activities** but are unsure if you need to do them yet, you can add them to your **Ideas List** for later. **Goals** and **Activities** can change anytime as you discover more about what you need and want to do.

The **Personal Scrum System** defines the **Events** where you plan the **Goals** and **Activities** you will carry out in the next period. The events create some regular space and time to plan your **Goals** & **Activities**.

At the **Weekly Planning Event**, you plan and forecast the **Activities** you will carry out during the next week. **Activities** are moved from the **To Do List** into the **This Week List** in your **Weekly Plan**. As part of this planning, you may add **Tasks** to help you further plan how to get the **Activities** done.

At the **Daily Planning Event**, you plan and forecast the **Activities** you will carry out during the next day. **Activities** are moved from the **This Week List** into the **Today List**. As part of this planning, you may add more **Tasks** as needed to help you plan.

The **In Progress List** holds the **Activities** you are currently and actively working on. The **On Hold List** will store the **Activities** that are waiting on someone or something else before you can continue doing them. The **Done List** is where **Activities** and **Goals** end up when they have been completed.

At the **Quarterly Planning Event**, you plan and forecast the **Goals** and **Activities** you plan to focus on in the next three months. As part of this, you will review the progress made over the past quarter, review your **Goals**, and change them as desired. The **Yearly Planning Event** serves the same purpose but ensures you are also planning across a more extended period and checking progress at a yearly level.

The **Ongoing Planning Event** is the ongoing activity of adding details to the **Ideas List** & **To Do List**.

The **Personal Scrum System** comprises 8 **Lists** and 5 **Events**. Unlike the Scrum framework upon which it is based, there are no defined roles. As the system is designed for individual use, the roles are redundant as you would have to fulfil them all.

Artifacts

Ideas List

Ideas List

The Ideas List is where we capture any ideas that come to us relating to our Goals and Activities. We all have great ideas, but few of us remember many of them, let alone act on them. Recording them as soon as you have them is a crucial practice to realise the benefit of working your subconscious mind. The subconscious constantly processes your experiences and can present insights our conscious mind is unaware of. Capturing these ideas when they bubble to the surface of our conscious mind can help us learn what we really want to do.

You should always note down any good idea that you have as soon as you have it and store it for later. Some people always keep a notepad and pencil close to hand for this purpose. I prefer to use a digital tool for this and the Notes app on my phone. Every so often, I transfer these ideas into my Ideas List. I prefer to use the Notes app on my phone in the first instance as it is a little faster, which makes recording the idea easier and, therefore, more likely to happen.

Recording notes is essential, but it can be inconvenient at times. I find that I have many of my best ideas when swimming. When I leave the pool and change, I always take time to note down any ideas that may be swirling around my mind. If I don't do this immediately, I will likely forget most of them. Recording these ideas as a habit takes discipline, but it is worth it. Great ideas often come to me when my mind is occupied with other things. Making the time to record them is essential. If we don't do this, it is equivalent to throwing money into a wallet and letting some of it fall onto the floor. You wouldn't do this with your money, so why would you do it with your valuable ideas?

Life is busy, and our attention is constantly switching between things. If we don't capture our ideas, many will be lost. These ideas don't need to be brilliant. Many of them will be ignored or discarded, but among these, there will be some nuggets of brilliance, and these are the ones we want to make sure we record and act on. To do this, we need a process to capture any ideas worth noting when they first appear.

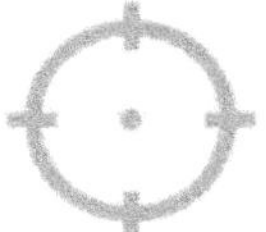

Goals List

The Goals List is where we store our currently active Goals. It should be a short list, perhaps as small as 1 item. Less is most certainly more when it comes to Goals. If you have too many active Goals, you will lose focus and delay progress.

It is OK to have future Goals that you are not actively working towards. These should be stored in the Ideas List, so it is clear they are ideas rather than active Goals.

To Do List

The To Do List is where we plan and store the Activities that we want to do in the future. It is an ordered list. The items at the top are what we will carry out in the short term. The items at the bottom are further in the future. The items at the bottom may never get done, as things may change before we get to them. In this case, they may be removed or pushed further down the To Do List as new essential items are added above them.

The ordering and contents of the To Do List can and should change as you discover more about the things you need to do to achieve your Goals and as the environment around you changes.

Wherever possible, we want to carry out high-value Activities and prioritise these accordingly on the To Do List. High-value Activities advance you toward your Goals, so they should be our primary focus and what we spend most of our time on. However, not all Activities are high value, but may still have to be done.

As previously mentioned, there are some things you just have to do as a human being who is part of modern society. Paying bills, replying to emails, arranging repairs, shopping for food, checking post. These are things you just have to do regularly to be part of the world.

If things are tiny and regular, I don't tend to add them to my To Do List. Things like checking the post and handling letters are just ongoing things that need to be done, so when I plan my weeks and days, I do it knowing there will be things like this that will require some time and attention. If, as part of this everyday Activity, a bigger Activity emerges, then I will add it to my To Do List (or even Weekly Plan if it needs more immediate attention) so I can plan it and act on it at some future point. My rule of thumb around this is that if something takes more than 30 minutes, it goes on the list to deal with at a future point.

This is a necessary strategy to stay focussed on the Activities that have been planned. Too many time-sapping distractions can be fatal to making real progress toward Goals. Not everything new is important or urgent, although it often feels that way. The human brain tends to value the new or novel over the old or known. This is something we must be aware of and resist.

Weekly Plan

The Weekly Plan is the output of the Weekly Planning event. The weekly plan includes:

- Weekly Goals - When selecting Goals, less is more. Select as few Goals as possible. If you consistently fail to achieve your Weekly Goals, you should reduce their number or scope in the coming weeks. I typically set 1-3 weekly Goals.
- Activities - These will be Activities selected from the top of the To Do List. Most but not all of these will support your Weekly Goals. Some things are not important in helping you achieve your Goals but just have to be done. E.g. paying bills, going shopping, or handling post. By selecting the Weekly Goals and Activities, we are creating a forecast for what we believe we will be able to complete in the week.
- A Plan of how to complete the Activities - This is typically represented as a list of tasks for each Activity. I don't aim for precision or detail when creating this plan. I want to identify the big tasks I need to do and then figure out the more minor details once I am doing Daily Planning or start working on the item.

The Weekly Plan should contain Goals and Activities that we forecast to be achievable in the week. Planning too much will be a waste of time and may serve to demotivate us if we do not achieve each milestone. Planning too little will mean we must revisit and plan again during the week. It is okay if we get it wrong, as things may change, and new invites or opportunities may emerge during the week. We should not fixate on this.

Humans tend to overestimate because we do not fully consider unknowns, so if in doubt, going smaller rather than larger is usually the best option. If we plan too little and finish early, we can always return to the To Do List and select some more Activities for the week.

A benefit of setting a realistic target is that we will get the endorphin hit from reaching our Goals by the end of the week. This sense of achievement can be a major factor in maintaining motivation as we work towards longer-term Goals.

This Week List

The This Week List is where we store the Goals & Activities that we plan to complete this week. It is an ordered list, and we start with the items at the top. The Goals sit at the top of the list, so we keep them in view throughout the week to know what we should focus on.

As we plan each day, Activities move from the This Week List to the Today List. If we manage to finish everything we plan for the week, the This Week List will be empty by the end of the week. If we do not manage to get everything done, then the contents will return to the To Do List during the next Weekly Planning event at the latest.

Today List

Today List

An updated Today List is the output of the Daily Planning event. The Daily Planning event takes place each day and allows you to spend time on Activities. This could be every day, every working day, or at the weekend when you are not at work and have time to focus on Activities.

During the Daily Planning event, you decide what Activities to carry out the next day. As part of this, you may spend time forecasting how long things might take and compare this to how much time you have available so that you select a realistic number of Activities. You also order the Activities to carry out the most important things first or when you are at your most productive. For most people, this will be at the start of the day. If you are unsure when you are most productive, schedule the most critical Activities first thing in the day. Getting the most important Activities done early in the day reduces stress and increases your sense of achievement, motivating you further.

If you run out of time, anything left in the Today List can be rolled over to tomorrow. This would never happen in a perfect world, but the world is not perfect, and with the best will in the world, we cannot always perfectly predict how long things will take or how much time we will have available to do them. I don't spend long on this or punish myself when I get it wrong. You will get better at forecasting this the more you do it. Some things are inherently unpredictable, so you will never be perfect when doing it. Accepting that, working on it and making progress while heading in the right direction is the best approach.

I plan my day by breaking it down into three parts - Morning, Afternoon and Maybe. I order the Activities so the most important things that require focus or a fresh mind go in the Morning. As the day moves on, I want to have completed the most important things first so that if my energy levels drop or something unexpected crops up, I can accept it, and it won't mean I have failed to achieve something significant. The Maybe part is for Activities I typically won't get to unless I make faster progress than expected.

Different types of Activities may also affect the order. When writing this book, I experimented and tried writing at other times. I found writing easier first thing in the Morning, so moving forward, I planned this as the first Activity of every day. I also found that I was best at admin tasks late in the day when I was lower on energy and favoured having something easy and unchallenging.

On other days, my motivation levels vary, and I move things around to get myself motivated and moving. Sometimes, if I am stuck, I prefer to re-order items and do something easy to overcome inertia. I can then move on to more important Activities once I am active.

In Progress List

Next to my Today List, I have an In Progress List. This is for Activities that I am actively doing right now. This will typically hold 1 (or a minimal number of) item(s). Working on too many things simultaneously slows you down and reduces the quality of what you do. This should be avoided wherever and whenever possible.

On Hold List

The On Hold List is where Activities are placed when you are waiting on someone or something to continue. If there is more you can do to advance in the activity, then it does not need to go onto the On Hold List. It is only for when there are no more tasks you can complete and you are waiting on someone or something.

The On Hold List is a necessary evil. In a perfect world, we would not need it. All the Activities we have to do would rely on us only, and we would never be dependent on someone or something else. But the real world is not like that.

The On Hold List helps us categorise and visualise the Activities we can go no further forward with. We should review it at Daily Planning to move anything you can out of it. If something has been unblocked, it should return to the This Week, Today, or even the To Do List if you don't plan to revisit it this week.

You should add a due date to items in the On Hold List that signals the date and time you expect the thing you are waiting on to materialise, thus allowing you to proceed. As part of Daily Planning, you can check the items on the On Hold List to see if any need to come back onto the Today List to be actioned.

If Activities have reached the On Hold List but are now unblocked, it is typically preferable to continue with this item rather than start something new. We have already invested time and effort into this, so we need to complete it to unlock the value it represents. Starting something new is easier than continuing with something that is already underway and has got stuck, but we need to resist the urge to start something and focus on finishing what we have already begun.

Done List

Done List

Done is the most important status. But the hardest one to reach. Finishing an Activity is more challenging than starting it. Anyone can start something and do the easy stuff. Having the discipline to persevere when obstacles arise or motivation declines is the only way to get to Done.

"Stop Starting, Start Finishing" - David J Anderson[1].

When deciding what to do in Daily Planning, the focus should be on the right-hand side of the Kanban Board and how to move In Progress or On Hold Activities forward and closer to Done.

Finishing is hard, to get there, we have to face up to and deal with the most challenging tasks that form part of the planned Activities. Moving something into the Done List results in a feeling of satisfaction that serves as a small psychological reward. It is also satisfying to look at the Done List at the end of a week and see it full of things you have accomplished.

Each week, our aim is to get Activities into the Done List. This moves us closer to our Goals and is what the Personal Scrum System is all about.

Planning Your Goals And Activities

The Personal Scrum System includes 5 Events where you plan your Goals and Activities.

Each Event happens regularly and at intervals defined in the Personal Scrum System. They ensure that you are frequently inspecting your progress, adapting your Goals & Activities, and replanning to take account of any changes or new insights.

Events

Weekly Planning

The Weekly Planning event occurs as close as possible to the start of each week. I prefer to do this on the preceding Friday afternoon before I finish the current week. Others choose to do this first thing on a Monday morning at the start of the new week.

Weekly Planning is where you set Weekly Goal(s) and select the Activities from the To Do List to support this, plus any other Activities that must be completed that week. These Goals & Activities are moved to the This Week List during Weekly Planning.

The recommended timebox for Weekly Planning is 1 hour. Weekly Planning typically takes me no more than 10 mins. I usually already have a To Do List with ready Activities at the top and an idea of what I would like to achieve that week. So, Weekly Planning involves pulling those Activities onto the This Week List, re-ordering it, and adding any tasks as needed.

A typical flow for Weekly Planning would be:

- Review what happened in the past week for any impacts on the next Weekly Plan.
- Set some Weekly Goals.
- Select Activities from the top of the To Do List to support these Weekly Goals.
- Select any other Activity items that have to be done this week.

- Plan (at least) 1 process improvement to make something faster/better/easier for you in future. This is a great practice to ensure that you are continuously improving.

Other tips for Weekly Planning:

- Activities should be broken down into half a day or less to help you better manage them and track your progress.
- If something is essential, block out calendar time to do it to ensure focus and limit distractions.
- Take into account your typical energy levels. I reserve Monday for easy Activities as I often experience low energy at the start of the week. I keep Friday afternoons (after I have prepared my Weekly Planning for the following week) for enjoyable Activities as a reward for the progress made during the week.

The result of the Weekly Planning event is the Weekly Plan artifact.

Daily Planning

The Daily Planning event is where you plan your Activities for the next day and add them to the Today List. As with Weekly Planning, you should be realistic about what you can achieve in a day. Take into account how many hours you expect to spend on Activities that day and other commitments that you may have. I do not use any formal estimation process to determine how many Activities might be possible in a day. I go with instinct and experience where possible.

The Daily Planning event can be held whenever it best suits you. For simplicity, it makes sense to do it at a consistent time each day. Many people prefer to do Daily Planning at the start of each day. I like to conduct Daily Planning at the end of each preceding day. For me, doing it at this time provides two essential benefits.

First, it brings the current working day to an end, which helps me disconnect from work and relax. By planning the next day at this point, I get to organise my thoughts and tie up any loose ends left open from the current day's Activities. By creating my plan for the next day, I get to move today's Activities out of my conscious mind and into the Weekly Plan, which leaves my brain free to focus on other non-work-related matters.

The other benefit of planning the next day the day before is that when you start working the next day, you know what you need to do without stopping to think about it. When I start working in the morning, I want to work on something of high value first while my brain is still fresh and my energy levels are high. I don't want to spend this important time planning, so doing it the night before lets me make a fast start while I am at my most productive and creative.

Daily Planning typically takes me no more than 5 minutes each day. The constituent parts for it are already in my Weekly Plan, so all I need to do is move things into the Today List, do some reordering, and potentially add some tasks.

Quarterly Planning

Each quarter, we should take time to look back at our Goals and assess our progress towards them. This is a crucial step as it is easy to lose sight of the Goals and drift away from them once the business of day-to-day life kicks in. Revisiting your Goals each quarter, checking your progress towards them, and replanning where required helps you re-focus on what matters most. Very often, reality has obliged me to diverge from my Yearly Plan. Some Goals may have been reached. Others I had intended to complete by this point may still be in progress or not yet started.

Quarterly Planning is an opportunity to replan and adjust your Goals, measures and dates. If the plan was too ambitious, and you expect the next quarters to be similar, then you may need to dial back your plan to reflect on what you have learned about what is possible. This is not a failure; it is an adaption based on learning.

Quarterly Planning must be carried out every three months. The specific timing is up to you. I conduct my Quarterly Planning in late December, March, June and September each year.

The output of Quarterly Planning is an updated set of Goals and an updated Ideas List & To Do List. These things can and will be updated at any other time. Taking time each quarter to do this helps ensure that you regularly step back and re-assess whether you are heading in the right direction, focussing on the right Goals, and carrying out suitable Activities to achieve those Goals.

Yearly Planning

At the end of each year, you should take some time to look back and review your progress against the Goals you set. This is also the time to set new Goals and adjust your existing Goals for the coming year.

You can carry out Yearly Planning whenever it makes sense to you. I like to do this in the relatively quiet time in late December between Christmas and New Year. The end of the year is when we naturally reflect on the past year and make plans for the coming one, so it feels like the right time to do this. For most people, work is also quiet at this time, and the volume of calls and emails declines, so it leaves some nice quiet time and space for reflection.

As part of Yearly Planning, I create a summary list of the Goals achieved, and the significant Activities completed this year. This serves two important purposes. Firstly, reflecting on what we have achieved reminds us of what is possible and helps to motivate us for the coming year. Secondly, it reminds us how much can be achieved in a year. Taking the time to reflect on the past year helps remind us what is possible if we set Goals and keep working towards them. I am often staggered by what I manage to achieve in a year. Looking back over the last year further reinforces the progress we can make if we stay focussed on our Goals.

Yearly Planning is an extension of the Quarterly Planning that I carry out simultaneously, but I take a little more time to reflect on the year past and the year ahead to focus beyond a single quarter.

Ongoing Planning

Ongoing Planning is the regular activity to refine the items in the Ideas List & To Do List. Each week, some time should be spent reviewing what has been added to these lists. You should ensure the items at the top of your To Do List have been refined to a ready state. By ready, we mean the things are small enough and well understood enough to be planned and completed within a week.

Ongoing Planning can be carried out at any point in the week when it makes sense to you, but you must do at least some of it. I tend to do it on Friday afternoons before I do Weekly Planning. I also revisit and refine the To Do List and Ideas List when things change, or new ideas emerge to reflect my latest understanding. Some weeks I do only a little Ongoing Planning. I do a lot on other weeks, which saves me time in the coming weeks. If this is done frequently, then Weekly Planning & Daily Planning become quicker and easier, which is what I aim for.

Ongoing Planning includes:

- Ensuring Activities are small enough and well understood enough to be completed in a week. Where they are not, they should be broken down into smaller Activities.
- Adding new or removing unnecessary Activities.
- Re-ordering Activities to reflect current priorities.

- Identifying any important dates related to Activities.
- Identifying dependencies between Activities and re-ordering the To Do List.
- Defining the tasks that will need to be carried out to complete the Activities. This is the focus of the Weekly Planning event, so only a little of this may be required in advance as part of Refinement.
- Carry out some rough sizing of Activities to aid future Weekly Planning decisions.

CHAPTER FIVE
Practices

Complementary Practices

The Personal Scrum System has enabled me to achieve Goals that I believed to be near impossible. It helps us develop superpowers. Most people move through life without much direction and do not set or meet most of their Goals. These people tend to remain unsatisfied with life. Being powerless to direct your life and being controlled by others and the system around you is rarely satisfying. Don't let it continue to happen to you.

In addition to the Personal Scrum System, there is a range of complementary practices that have proved vital in helping me reach my Goals. In the next section, I will share those practices with you.

Learning

As a child, I was fascinated by Superheroes and their powers and abilities. I always dreamed of having superpowers and being able to do incredible feats with them. Of course, I knew that this was all pure fantasy and no one had superpowers. One day, I realised that this is not true, and all of us are capable of developing superpowers that will give us an advantage in life.

The ability to learn is a superpower that anyone can develop. If you get good at learning, you can pick up new knowledge, skills, and abilities that you can put to work to help you achieve your Goals.

Traditional University education is aimed at helping us build this capability. However, many people manage to graduate with some knowledge in their chosen subject but are unable or unwilling to continue learning by themselves.

Many people see education as something you do when you are young and when you get sent on a course at work. If you see learning like this, you will have a much narrower field of knowledge, which will put you in a risky position in the long run. The rate of change in the world is accelerating. For most people, the job you do and the skills you need will be very different in 5-10 years. It is estimated that most people will have 12 jobs during their lifetime. Since starting their first job after University/College, 29% of people have completely changed fields[1].

If you cannot continue to learn new skills, you may find yourself in a dying industry or with a redundant skillset. As a result, you will have limited prospects and eventually find yourself unemployed or unemployable.

Conversely, if you learn "how to learn" and exercise the skill daily, you will open a world of opportunities. Every new thing you know gives you an advantage in life and against your competitors (should you have any). The knowledge you accumulate will also compound. Many of the things you learn will relate to other things and open up possibilities that you could not have previously imagined.

Here are some examples of superpowers I have developed by learning new things over the years:

- Website Development - I saw that websites were important and taught myself to build them. This helped me land a better job early in my career. When I started my training company, it meant I could create a website without spending huge amounts and have the skills and knowledge to create the website I actually wanted.
- Search Engine Marketing - By reading a few well-reviewed books, I learned to market my products at the lowest possible cost without spending massive amounts to have someone do it for me.
- Accounting - In the past, you may have needed a bookkeeper and accountant to do many things for your business. Now, with some basic knowledge and a suitable tool, you can do 95% of this at almost no cost.
- Sales - I am not a salesperson and have had no formal training. I read a few of the best reviewed books on this subject and picked up 80% of the knowledge you need to be a good salesperson.
- Writing/Publishing - I had no experience writing blog posts or books. By reading some books on the subject, I learned the basics of writing and publishing, making it possible to create this book.

- Social Media Management - I discovered a low-cost tool that lets me create, schedule, and automate my social media marketing. I have used this successfully for 5+ years, requiring only 1 hour every three months to manage. This would cost £1,000s if I were to pay someone else.

For a small business, all the small costs add up. It can be worth paying people to do these things for you, but when you start, you typically don't have the resources to do so. Doing it yourself and automating it can allow you to get started with minimal investment and save you vast amounts of money as you grow. At some point down the line, you can choose which things you should hold onto and which things you should pay someone to take over for you. Knowing how to do these tasks yourself gives you tremendous advantages when the time comes to do this.

The good news is that there are many sources of learning:

- Training Courses - When I seek instructor-led learning, I always look for the best Trainers who lead their fields. They charge more, but if you invest time and money, you want to learn from the best. Trying to save in this area is a false economy. Invest in yourself and get the best training possible.
- Daily Reading - News, Blogs - I use an RSS reader (Feedly) and a Read Later tool (Pocket) to curate news and information from a wide range of sources I am interested in. On a typical day, I review more than 300 pieces and read up to 50 of them at some level. I do this every day, no matter what. This means that I am learning more about the topics that interest me every day. This learning compounds over time and leads to deep expertise in various subjects. As my interests change, I adjust the sources.
- Books - Find the best books in the subject area you are

interested in. Create a backlog of books to read and start buying and reading. Most books are £10 or less, and the value you can gain from them is massively more than this small investment. It can be hard to find the time to read books, and this is something I struggle with. I currently make time to read on a Sunday, but find it hard to pick up where I left off after seven days.

- eBooks - Using eBooks over traditional paper books means you are always carrying all your books and can read them whenever you have some free time. You can also read the free previews to decide whether to invest in the whole book. Amazon also has many specialist short books that can be a great way to pick up some expert knowledge quickly and at a low cost. This book is an example of that. I have condensed over 20 years of my professional experience and knowledge into something you can buy for a small amount of money and read in a few hours. The value you will gain when you act on the recommendations it contains will represent a fantastic return on your investment.

Investing in yourself is the best investment you can make. It is better than almost any other investment, as what you learn will pay you back daily for the rest of your life. It will increase your ability to reach your Goals, whatever they may be.

Learning is a superpower. Become your own superhero and develop the ability to learn. Get good at learning new things, and you will dramatically increase your chances of succeeding at whatever you set your mind to.

Focus

Once you have worked out what to do and have started doing it, it is vital to stay focused, work efficiently, and avoid distractions. Focus is essential to get things done and achieve your Goals.

Limiting distractions is critical. The modern world is full of things that demand our time and distract us.

- Phone calls.
- Messages via Email, Slack, WhatsApp, or SMS.
- News from various sources, including TV, radio, and websites.
- Social Media - Facebook, Twitter, Instagram, LinkedIn.
- Talking to colleagues and friends.

The possible distractions are endless and will overwhelm us if we allow them. It is perfectly possible to spend any available time you have servicing these distractions and watching hours, days, weeks, months, and years rush past as we stay busy but achieve very little and fail to work towards our Goals.

The difficulty is that many or most of these things cannot be ignored, so we have to find a way to deal with them whilst still leaving the majority of our time free to focus on high-value Activities that will help us achieve our Goals. Here are some techniques that can help you to do this:

Silence your phone

Silence your phone (except for the most important people - boss, partner, main client etc.). The phone allows anyone to contact you at any time. While this is wonderful, it is a huge source of distraction that will waste vast amounts of your time. If you answer the phone every time it rings, you place other people's needs above your own. And few people are genuinely more important than you are. If you allow constant interruptions, you will struggle to find time to focus on work and enter a flow state where you are fully concentrating. Even short tasks that should take an hour could end up taking days. The quality of what you do will also decline if you allow constant interruptions to break your focus.

I only allow alerts for calls and messages from a tiny group of people. For everyone else, I check my phone periodically and respond at a time to suit me. For calls from clients, I use a tool to share my calendar and allow people to book a time for a call or meeting. By automating this process, I avoid all the back-and-forth messages that would be needed to arrange meetings and ensure they happen at a time that suits me, when they do not interrupt other important work.

I make 2x 3-hour windows available each week on a Monday and Wednesday late afternoon for this purpose. This means all my important calls are batched together, so I can get into call mode and focus and give this vital Activity my full attention.

Control Your Email

Email is essential for many jobs today, but it is a potentially huge source of distraction. If you are not careful, you may spend all day responding to emails and get no high-value work done.

My strategy with email is to limit the times I check it. I aim to check and reply to emails no more than three times a day; at the start of the day, around lunchtime and before I finish for the day. Other people check a little more often or as rarely as once daily. Plan a schedule that allows you to be responsive enough but gives you long periods without distractions to focus on meaningful work.

Work Somewhere Distraction Free

Make sure you have a place that is free from distraction and conducive to work. For some people, this is an office with a door they can close. For others, this is a coffee shop where they work with headphones and music. Make people nearby aware of how you work and when interruptions would be welcomed or not, and remind them when they forget.

People who don't work this way may not appreciate or respect your rules. But most people minimise their work and achieve little, and these people are another source of distraction. If you want to be successful and achieve your Goals, you will have to push back when people ignore your requests. Don't let other people steal your time and prevent you from achieving your Goals.

Manage Your Internet Access

The internet is fantastic and gives us access to vast amounts of information that can help us achieve great things, but it can also be a massive distraction. It is easy to slip into a routine of checking the news, Facebook or Instagram every 30 mins and waste a lot of time that could be better spent elsewhere. The attention economy that these websites are part of, makes their money by taking your time and attention. Don't be a victim. Take control of your attention.

Some people decide not to check these things during the working day to limit distraction. I limit myself to checking them as a small reward when I complete some valuable work and save most of my reading and reviews of sources for after work. Come up with a strategy that works for you and stick to it to free yourself from wasteful distractions.

Save Your Reading For Later

The internet is such a potential distraction because it provides an endless source of content to read. Reading takes time, energy and attention away from your important work. A strategy I would recommend to help manage this is to store and save that reading for later.

I recommend using a tool called Pocket, which allows you to quickly and easily save articles for a more appropriate moment. It also allows you to read on any device you choose and even offline if necessary. I save content throughout the day and then allocate some time to catch up with my reading at the end of each day. I leave longer content for the weekend when I have more time and some content I only catch up with at the end of each month.

I find this approach invaluable as it lets me stay focussed on high-value Activities during the day, but not lose important content that I want to read later. This allows me to save valuable brain processing time for Activities that advance me towards my Goals.

Calendar Blocking

Calendar blocking involves assigning timeboxes during your day to essential Activities and scheduling them in your calendar. By assigning Activities to pre-scheduled timeboxes in your calendar, you can more easily avoid distractions and stay focused.

Once the Activity is assigned to your calendar, you have created the mental space to act on it. It clarifies your most crucial Activity during this time, and as a result, you are more likely to focus on it and get it done. As it is on your calendar, it will also prevent anyone else from booking a meeting at this time.

Silence Your Notifications

Silence your phone, email and other notifications and only check and respond at pre-defined times. This is a practice I have used for many years, and it is a game changer. If you answer your phone every time it rings or pings, you will be constantly distracted and stressed and have little time to do high-value Activities that require focus. You are allowing other people to set your schedule and placing their needs above your own, which is unhealthy and will drastically reduce your productivity.

Whenever a phone rings or beeps, there is someone who wants something from you. Why should their needs take precedence over the plans you have made for today and the Activities that you are currently doing? They shouldn't, with a few minor exceptions (your spouse, child, boss, and biggest client). But even these people should understand you won't answer/respond at all times. If it is urgent, they should make that clear so you know to prioritise it.

Flow State

The ability to focus for hours, days, and even weeks at a time is critical if you want to make meaningful progress towards your Goals. If you allow frequent interruptions, your brain will never get into a flow state, and progress will be slow and painful.

The concept of flow state was popularised by psychologists Mihaly Csikszentmihalyi and Jeanne Nakamura[1]. The flow state is where you become fully immersed in whatever you do. When you're giving your fullest attention to an Activity you are singularly focused on and engaged in, you may experience a flow state. This is a state where the usual chatter of the mind fades away, and all that matters is your Activity.

Time flies when you work in a flow state and make meaningful progress. The work will be enjoyable, even if it is challenging. This is where the magic happens and where real progress is made. People who get good at avoiding distractions and entering a flow state typically seem to get huge amounts done and make massive progress in life.

Their focus appears to give them a productivity superpower. In reality, anyone can develop this skill, but it will take practice and patience to make this an unconscious habit.

If you struggle with focus, it often means you are not genuinely motivated by the Goal you have set. The Goal you are working towards is likely the wrong Goal. However, it is equally possible that you have the right Goal, but it is far enough in the distance that it doesn't serve to motivate and cause you to focus. This is where having Intermediate Goals can help. A shorter-term Goal that serves as a stepping stone toward the larger Goal will seem more achievable. The payoff will be sooner, and the good feeling that you get from reaching the Intermediate Goal will serve to keep you moving forward towards the larger Goal.

Even if you are committed to your Goal, it can still be challenging to avoid the myriad distractions that will emerge to demand your time each day. It is easy to get stuck in the minutiae and be busy doing stuff, but not move closer to your Goals. Entering a flow state can also be challenging if the Activity is not enjoyable, too easy, or too hard. It is not always possible to enter a flow state. But the more aligned our Goals and Activities are with what we want to do, the more frequently we might experience it.

How to enter a flow state:

1. Do something you love - This is the easiest way to get into a flow state. Your brain will take you there automatically.

2. Create a routine - Create a series of actions you do every time you're about to begin your Activity. This could be a short walk, a coffee, or going to a specific location. Following a routine will get your brain used to and ready for a flow state.

3. Pick one crucial Activity - Achieving a flow state is best accomplished while focusing on one major Activity requiring a significant portion of brain power. Avoid multitasking completely.

4. Eliminate distractions - Focus on creating an environment with minimal distractions. Silence any notifications or other sources of potential distraction, such as your phone or email.

5. Identify your peak times - Identify the times when your mind most naturally functions at its best. For many people, this is first thing in the morning.

Focusing on the day's main task during these times will make the flow state more achievable.

The next superpower (Prioritisation) can make a big difference with this.

Prioritisation

The next superpower you can develop is prioritisation. The ability to prioritise successfully is vital in our busy world. There is always an unlimited number of Goals you could set and Activities you could do. Ideas are free, and your options are limitless. But the time and resources you have at your disposal are limited.

We have perhaps 40 hours at work to get things done each week and a few hours each weekend. We also have a range of commitments we need to service each week to survive, stay healthy, and provide for our family. The time many of us are left with to pursue our Goals is often severely limited. This means we need to make hard conscious choices about which Goals we set and what Activities we take on to achieve them.

Many of the most successful people do not take on massive amounts and work long hours. The more we do, the luckier we get, but also the more energy we expend, and this energy will eventually deplete, and we may burn out. The most successful people are the ones who are good at setting a limited number of Goals and saying no to anything else that may distract them. They will then be highly selective about the Activities they take on to work towards those Goals. The people who are the best at recognising the opportunities that should be turned down and the Activities that should not be done usually make the fastest progress and achieve their Goals.

If we take on too much, we are destined to fail. We need to

carefully pick the opportunities we want to pursue. This will inevitably mean saying no, or not now, to many interesting and exciting opportunities. But if we take on everything that looks good, our progress in most areas will halt. Many people fall into this trap and bounce from one thing to the next without ever making any meaningful progress towards anything.

Perseverance

Making real, lasting progress toward your Goals will take time. There will be many distractions along the way that offer faster, easier rewards. Perseverance is vital to achieving your Goals.

Many people spend their life distracted by Activities that provide immediate rewards. Drinking alcohol offers an immediate reward to our brains. Working in a sales job where we get a monthly bonus if we meet our targets provides a near immediate reward. Immediate rewards can distract us from our longer-term and harder-to-reach Goals. Many spend their entire lives taking the immediate reward and never achieve their longer-term Goals.

To make real progress towards long-term Goals, we need to be able to persevere. We need to be able to keep going, even if there is no immediate reward or gratification. Setting short-term Goals can help with this as it will provide us with a regular feeling of accomplishment which can help to keep us motivated for the long haul. But sometimes, to reach a big Goal, we will have to do lots of Activities that will take a long time, and there will be no significant rewards along the way. Patience and perseverance are essential if we are to get there.

Most people give up when things get challenging, or easier options with faster gratification emerge. You will need to develop patience and perseverance to reach your longer-term Goals. The Personal Scrum System can help with this. It encourages us to plan in short cycles.

Focusing on small incremental progress toward our Goals and making the results visual, even if it is a tick in a box or a card in the Done List, can help us see that we are making progress, and this can help keep us moving forwards. In Quarterly Planning, you can also reflect on how much you have achieved and how closer you are to your Goals, which can aid motivation.

Breaking big Activities down into smaller ones, and big strategic Goals into smaller intermediate Goals makes it far more likely we will keep going. Big things look impossible and serve to demotivate us. When we break big things into smaller ones, those smaller things seem more achievable and can make them all seem possible. We will eventually achieve the big things if we do enough of these small things. It is simple in theory, but not so easy in practice, and perseverance is essential so that we keep going and do not give up when the going gets tough.

We also need to develop the ability to persevere, despite uncertainty. We may set long-term Goals and never be sure if they are possible or the "right" Goals until we achieve them, which may be many years later.

When I set out to become a Scrum.org Professional Scrum Trainer, I didn't know if it was the right Goal for me. Did I want to be a Trainer? Could I be a good trainer? Could I afford to take the risk of not earning as much while I developed these new skills? I was plagued with doubt along the way and often thought of giving up.

In the end, I doubled down on my efforts. I decided to complete it as fast as possible. Doubling down helped keep me motivated. By going all in, progress was quicker, and I could better focus and reach my Goal sooner. A single Goal will be achieved much faster than many Goals being worked on simultaneously. Your focus will be better, and your motivation will stay higher.

A mistake many people make is to look at successful people and imagine that the success was quickly or easily achieved. In most cases, this is not true. Success often takes time, and there are rarely shortcuts.

The co-creators of Scrum, Ken Schwaber and Jeff Sutherland, were 50 & 54, respectively, when they shared Scrum with the world in 1995. It would be ten years before Scrum began to be widely adopted and another ten years before many millions of people were using it globally. Ken and Jeff had enjoyed long careers before they created Scrum, and it was a long journey to where they are today.

Stan Lee created his first hit comic, "The Fantastic Four," just before his 39th birthday in 1961. He had been making comics for many years with limited success and was close to quitting. In the years that followed, he co-created the now legendary Marvel Universe, whose characters such as Spider-Man and the X-Men have become cultural icons.

Samuel L. Jackson has been among the biggest Hollywood stars for years now. The films he has appeared in have collectively grossed over $27 billion worldwide, making him the highest-grossing actor of all time. Before landing an award-winning role at age 43 in Spike Lee's film "Jungle Fever" in 1991, he had only managed bit parts, despite being an actor for over a decade.

So the good news is that it is fine if you haven't made it yet. There is still time, and it is never too late, as long as you keep working towards your Goals.

Timeboxing

Parkinson's Law states that work expands to fill the time allotted for completion. Cyril Northcote Parkinson first coined the term in a humorous essay he wrote for The Economist in 1955[1].

This is especially true when the work is complex. That is, there is a high degree of unknowns, change and uncertainty. Writing, programming, designing and planning are often complex Activities where the amount of time spent on an Activity can vary from a little to a lot.

So how do we prevent spending ever-increasing amounts of time on complex work? One effective way to control this is to use the practice of timeboxing. Timeboxing means setting a fixed amount of time for a particular task or Activity. Whilst you are not guaranteed to finish the task within the time allocated, the timebox brings focus and increases the probability of making some progress.

Some further benefits of timeboxing:

- You will start working on tasks more readily if you know it will only be for a relatively short period.
- You reduce the likelihood of procrastination by creating focused time. Timeboxing forces focus to some degree, and this is potentially powerful.
- More easily set, strict limits on how much time you'll spend on a specific task or Activity.

- Boost your productivity. The timebox provides a sense of urgency which can help to increase productivity.
- Deal with the need for perfectionism and the over-processing and over-doing of tasks.
- If you need other people to work with you, you can set clear and agreed expectations around the time commitment required.
- Help you plan a better working rhythm.

If you complete the Activity before the timebox expires, you can end it early.

The Pomodoro Technique

Another helpful technique to help you maintain focus when working is the Pomodoro technique. This builds on the concept of timeboxing (mentioned in the earlier chapter).

You break your work period into 25-minute chunks separated by five-minute breaks. These intervals are referred to as Pomodoros. After around four Pomodoros, you take a longer break of approximately 15 minutes. Relatively short working periods with regular breaks can be an effective way to maintain focus and eliminate procrastination.

I use the Pomodoro technique when I need to do something, but I find myself procrastinating and making slow progress. I know other people who use it for a few hours each day and find that they can achieve what may have otherwise taken them most of the day in a few hours.

It can take a little time and discipline to use Pomodoros, but for many people, the results are well worth the small investment.

You can use many tools to help you use the Pomodoro technique, which can be found in the *"How To Start Using The Personal Scrum"* section at the end of the book.

The 80/20 Rule

The 80/20 rule (also known as the Pareto principle[1]) is a phenomenon that states that roughly 80% of outcomes come from 20% of causes. While it doesn't always come to be an exact 80/20 ratio, this imbalance is often seen worldwide in many domains.

Italian economist Vilfredo Pareto developed the Pareto principle in 1896. Pareto observed that 80% of the land in Italy was owned by only 20% of the population. He also witnessed this happening with plants in his garden, where 20% of his plants bore 80% of the fruit.

Some further examples of the 80/20 rule:

- 80% of a company's profits come from 20% of its customers[2]
- The richest 20% of the world's population receive 82.7% of the world's income.[3]
- Microsoft noted that by fixing the top 20% of the most-reported bugs, 80% of the related errors and crashes in a given system would be eliminated[4]
- In health care in the United States, in one instance approximately 20% of patients have been found to use 80% of health care resources[5]

While the 80/20 rule applies in many contexts, it is a helpful complimentary practice for the Personal Scrum System. It can help you to determine where to focus your efforts to help you achieve your Goals. Prioritise the 20% of Goals that will help you achieve your desired success. Prioritise the 20% of Activities that will produce the best results and move you towards your chosen Goals.

There are only so many minutes in an hour, hours in a day, and days in a week. The 80/20 rule can help you focus on the things that matter instead of chasing endless opportunities and burning yourself out.

Inbox Zero

Managing email can become a full-time job and a massive distraction if you don't have a strategy to handle it. Managing emails takes time and effort. Frequently staring at an enormous list of emails or searching through them will add stress and waste time. Managing email creates a cognitive overhead that is best minimised or avoided.

My preferred strategy for preventing this is called Inbox 0. This is a simple but not necessarily easy system where at all times, you strive to keep the number of emails in your Inbox to 0. Now I don't mind if the emails in my Inbox build up while I am not looking at it. But when I check my Inbox, my Goal is to process every email in that visit.

- If you can read and archive it without a response, then do so.
- If it is something quick (< 5 minutes), deal with it at the time and reply immediately.
- If it is Spam, mark it as Spam, so no more comes through from the same source in future.
- If it is an unwanted sales or marketing message, unsubscribe so you don't have to hear from them again.
- If it is non-urgent and non-important, snooze it for an unspecified future time. Create some space to come back to these snoozed messages and deal with them.

- If it will take a long time to handle the email, add it to your To Do List or Weekly Plan so you can handle it alongside the other Activities at a planned time.

Sending emails at the right time can also reduce the volume of emails you have to deal with. Sometimes it is best to schedule a reply for a few hours later or even the next day if you know the recipient is likely to reply again. By providing a clear answer a little later, when they have moved on to something else, you may be able to avoid receiving another email. Slowing conversations down can be effective in reducing the volume of the conversation. When someone emails you late on a Friday, scheduling your reply for first thing Monday morning may avoid everyone involved getting into an email conversation over the weekend.

If you are fortunate enough to have someone you can call on to help you manage your emails - do it! Once I got busier as a Trainer, I could no longer keep up with the volume of emails I received. My first employee was tasked with taking this on for me. My workload increased for the first few weeks as I was teaching them how to do it. But once they got the hang of it, my workload reduced significantly, leaving me more time to focus on high-value work that adds to my business. Consider finding someone to do this if you want to save time and stay focussed. This Activity can be outsourced to someone else at a low cost, and the time you save can be spent working towards your Goals.

Make use of pre-written responses to save you typing the same things over and over again. Even after I had passed much of my email to an assistant, there were still some emails that I had to handle myself. I looked for patterns in the replies and created pre-written responses that I could use when possible. These can save significant time and energy and make managing emails easier. It also makes the replies a higher quality as I can ensure I say the right things each time rather than relying on my memory to remember what to say.

Finding a good email application is vital. Something that

works across all your computers, phones and other devices, syncs your settings and allows you to manage multiple accounts is critical. Basic and essential functionality like Snoozing, Scheduling, Signatures, Canned Responses and Search can all save vast amounts of time and energy.

Touch It Once

When work is coming at you from all sides, it's easy to get distracted and lose focus on your most essential Activities and Goals. A particularly wasteful form of procrastination is when we frequently revisit some Activity, spending some short time looking at it without making significant progress.

The solution is following the Touch It Once rule. As soon as you touch an Activity, be it an email, a letter, or a request from a colleague, you immediately act on it. This could be fully completing the task or adding it to your To Do List or Weekly Plan for later attention. As a rule of thumb, do it right away if it takes less than five minutes. If it takes more than five minutes, add it to a list for later. Once you've done it or planned it, you can safely let go of it and focus on the planned high-value Activity you should be doing and give it your full attention again.

Following this strategy will save you time and prevent your brain from spending precious resources on these Activities. The more you revisit the Activity item, the more it will sit at the back of your brain, nagging away at you and drawing your attention away from other more critical Activities. Dealing with it immediately or logging it for later allows your brain to let go and stay focused on the planned Activity.

Maintaining focus in today's busy, distraction-filled world is a vital skill to develop. Following the Touch It Once rule, like most of the tips recommended in this book, ultimately comes down to discipline. But once you establish this time-saving habit, it will become automatic.

Getting Started

If you can't start with what you want to do first, start with something, even if it is something small and manageable. Sometimes, you must overcome the inertia to move on to more important work later. There is nothing wrong with this. Accept it and work with it.

I start work soon after waking up and am often still drowsy. Some days I can immediately move into high-value work and get lots done. On other days I struggle to start, and when I feel this happening, I switch to a small and simple task to get me moving. Most of the time, I can move on to high-value planned work a short time later.

Some days, your brain only feels like doing certain things, and no amount of task switching will resolve this. Sometimes the brain wants to do a specific type of work only. Fighting it can work on occasions, but at other times, it is better to follow your instinct, accept that today is not the day for high-value work and use the time to do low-value work that needs to get done.

Pay attention to the times of day when you feel you perform at your best. Do your most important work then and save the low-value work for other times. I'm at my most productive around 30 mins after waking up. I usually start with some easy work to start and then quickly switch to work on the essential things of the day. On a good day, I like to have completed my most important work by lunch, leaving me the afternoon for lower value (but still often essential) work like replying to emails, meeting with clients, or planning.

I also find I am highly productive early in the morning before other people are awake. However, I have never been an early riser, so I struggle to get up so early on an ongoing basis. Instead, I reserve this as a technique to get important work done. If something is challenging and important that I need to do, I will set an alarm to get me up early so I can work on it before anyone else wakes up and the distractions of the day start to flow in.

Set up your working space in a way that helps your mental functioning. If you focus better with music on, have it on. If need be, use earphones. If you think best on your feet, work standing up or walk around frequently. I prefer a tidy working environment with little about to distract me. I keep my desk clutter-free. I like a little background music. I listen to the same radio station daily, which plays classic hits from the past. I know every song, so it is not distracting and serves as a comfort during the working day.

I have a small home office with a desk, computer, office chair and importantly, a door I can close. This helps me to ignore anything else going on at home while I am working so I do not get distracted. I did not do my best work in an open-plan office many years ago. Fortunately, I'll never have to work in those environments again.

Another technique I occasionally use is going to a public place like a coffee shop to work around other people. Sometimes being around other people provides new energy and can help me progress on something I am stuck on. When I do this, I find I make much more meaningful progress in a short time.

Many self-help books focus on the need for increased productivity. Finding ever more creative ways to get more things done. I used to follow this advice. I packed my days full of work to get as much done as possible.

I found that over time I became more and more tired. And not just the apparent form of tiredness where your body and mind cry out for rest and sleep. This also included a more pervasive and damaging, long-term, underlying fatigue. This long-term tiredness made everything I tried to do slower and more difficult. It robbed me of creative thought and left me short-tempered and challenging to work with or be around.

Eventually, I realised through long and painful experience that I was focussing on the wrong thing. Instead of focusing on getting more done, I needed to focus on making sure I was doing the right things. We need to find ways to work out what Goals and Activities are worth pursuing and eliminate or defer the rest of the things we could do.

Goals and Activities are limitless. You could sit for 1 hour and develop a list of Goals and related work that would take more than the rest of your life to complete. Conversely, our ability to work and reach Goals is severely limited. Most of us can only work 40 hours a week on average. If you are employed, then these hours will belong to your employer. Family, friends and leisure will take another portion of your time, leaving you potentially only a small amount of time each week to pursue any Goals you have for yourself.

If we take on too much, the progress will be slow, results will be delayed, and motivation will suffer. If we move too slowly towards our Goals, then as things around us change, our Goals may need to change before we have made any significant progress towards them.

It is incorrect to say that maximising your work does not help. The more work you do, the luckier you will get, as you can afford to do more wrong things and still be successful. However, it is not a long-term sustainable approach and should be saved as a technique that you deploy only when unique, high-value, and time-bound opportunities arise. I sometimes worked long hours and weekends when setting up my business as it was necessary to seize some short-term opportunities. I was always conscious that this was a short-term strategy that I would stop as soon as possible.

Overloading ourselves and being busy all the time is a poor strategy. It will lower our long-term energy levels and stifle our creativity. If there is no pleasure in working towards our Goals, then it may not be worth it in the long run. Leisure and rest are vital to maintaining progress towards Goals. Life is a Marathon, not a Sprint.

The answer to all this is to ruthlessly limit and prioritise the Goals we set and the Activities we will carry out to achieve them. The secret to success is not how fast you do things, it is choosing and doing the right things continuously over long periods. Being as efficient as possible at doing something is also essential, and the Personal Scrum System is designed to enable all of this.

Making the right choices about your Goals and Activities is not easy. You have to make judgement calls about the future, which is uncertain and unpredictable. The good news is that the more you do it, the better you get at it. The more Goals you achieve, the better you will get at setting and achieving the right Goals in future. The more you do, the more you learn and the "luckier" you will get with your choices.

Knowing When To Quit

Setting Goals and making meaningful progress towards them is a marathon, not a sprint. As we do the work necessary to achieve them, the world around us will change. We will learn more about ourselves, what we want, and our Goals as time passes. One consequence is that our circumstances and desires may vary, meaning the Goals we have set may no longer be appropriate.

Our Goals can and will change. That is normal and OK. We need to recognise when this happens so we do not continue working towards something we no longer want or need. Our subconscious will intuit if we do this, and motivation will decline, and progress will slow. If we don't recognise this we risk spending significant time and resources working toward the wrong Goal. This will mean we are not spending that time and those resources moving toward the new Goals we may have not yet identified. We need to learn when to stop and when to change direction.

Many people struggle with this due to the Sunk Cost Fallacy. This is our tendency to follow through on any Goal if we have already invested resources into achieving it, regardless of whether the current and future costs outweigh the benefits.

A sunk cost is a past cost. One that cannot be recovered. Something buried deep in the human psyche makes it hard for us to give up on something when we have already invested in it, even if the potential benefit is now low or even negative. Continuing to work towards the Goal will ensure the investment was not wasteful. However, if the future value is low or negative, it is better to accept the waste and move on.

The Goal was set during different times, and things have now changed. This is an inevitable reality of life and one we need to learn to accept. We won't achieve all our Goals because we shouldn't continue working toward Goals that won't take us where we want to be. The associated waste is the cost of discovering our new Goals, which should be accepted and celebrated.

Here is a classic example of the sunk cost fallacy. You head to a casino to win big money. After a few hours in the casino, you are on a bad streak and have lost much of your money. You may believe that since you have already lost so much, you should continue gambling the rest to recover your losses. The past losses have no bearing on the future likelihood of winning (or losing). The past losses are a sunk cost.

The Goal After The Goal

As human beings, we need something to stimulate the mind and work towards. We need something to struggle against to feel happy and fulfilled when we achieve it.

Success is not something you can achieve and then rest and retire. Our Goals, once completed, must be replaced with new ones. The feeling of satisfaction from achieving a Goal does not last.

For many years, my Goal was to become a successful Trainer who ran a regular schedule of public Scrum training courses. This was a significant strategic Goal that took many years of sustained effort. I got there in time, but there was no single moment when the Goal was achieved. I only realised at my Yearly Planning that it had been reached. When I set it, this was a milestone that I thought could be impossible and was far beyond my comfort level or experience. When I set that Goal, I thought that if I achieved it, my professional life would be complete, and I could rest a little, safe in the knowledge of my achievement. Of course, when I got there, this was no longer true. I had changed as a person as I worked towards that Goal. I was no longer the person that saw that as enough. When I got there, I realised I would need to set a new Goal to keep myself motivated and happy. This book represents one of the new Goals I set at that point.

Set The Goal After The Goal Now!

* * *

Another helpful practice when setting Goals is to consider the Goal after the Goal. You can do this when you set the first Goal or at any other point as you move towards that Goal. The reality of doing valuable work is that the effort needed to achieve it will often be significant and much more than you initially realise.

The Scrum training courses include an assessment and certification that students take after completion. For many years, students asked me for more help with these assessments and wanted materials to help them practice.

I eventually set a Goal to create practice assessments to help with this. I realised I could give it for free to my students. The first measure of success was that it would help my students gain their certification, increase the value of my courses relative to other providers, and increase satisfaction for my students.

The second measure was that I could charge a small fee for access to the practice assessment for other people who had not taken my course, and it would become another revenue stream for my training business. There were many good reasons to do this.

It was a significant amount of work that took much longer than I expected. These are some of the things I had to do along the way:

- Create a Learning Management System for my website.
- Write questions, answers and feedback.
- Design graphics and images for the web pages.
- Write copy for the landing page for the assessment.
- Enable free or paid access to the practice assessments.
- Train my support team on how everything worked relating to all of this.

Once I launched the practice assessment, I found I was correct in my estimation of its value for my existing students. For most, it proved a significant benefit and was very popular. I received feedback that the practice assessment helped people pass the actual assessment and gain certification.

However, I quickly realised that I was still some way from achieving my 2nd measure. People who had not been to my courses were not purchasing the practice assessments, even though I knew it was valuable because many people had told me. I realised that as well as building the practice assessments, I would also need to market them. There was a Goal beyond the Goal that I needed to now work towards.

On the one hand, if I had known about the Goal beyond the Goal, I may not have started in the first place, as my lack of experience in marketing may have put me off. As it was, I had developed a great product with proven value, so I was not motivated to set new Goals and continue forward. However, my next Goal would be to market the practice assessments and generate sales. An intermediate Goal to get there would be to learn about and experiment with marketing.

Set Intermediate Goals

Setting big, far-off, and ambitious Goals is vital to making the hard work required bearable. The big Goal and achievements we can see off in the distance help to keep us motivated. Smaller intermediate Goals that move us towards the big strategic Goal are essential to give us a feeling of achievement along the way and help us see and measure progress. If a Goal is too far off with no milestones along the way, we may lose interest and motivation before we get there.

When I set myself a strategic Goal to write this book, I realised it would take many sustained months of work, and I would risk losing motivation. As a result, I set some intermediate Goals and Measures along the way. My intermediate Goals and measures were:

- Write 1000 words a day, at least five days a week.

- Finish the first draft, first & second edits, and images in the 1st quarter.
- Finish all edits by the end of the 2nd quarter.

This is also effective as it sends a message to your subconscious that you will achieve the first Goal because you are already thinking about what comes next.

SMART Goals

SMART Goals[1] are specific, measurable, achievable, relevant and time-based. SMART describes a set of criteria that are frequently applied to Goals, asserting that goals should be:

- Specific – target a specific area for improvement. Avoid making the Goal too broad.
- Measurable – include an indicator of progress that you can track as you progress.
- Achievable – realistic, even if it is difficult and far off.
- Relevant – the right Goals to help you achieve the success you want.
- Time-based – specify when the result(s) will be achieved.

Using SMART goals can help ensure the Goals you set are useful in helping you make meaningful progress.

Limit Work In Progress

Do not take on too much work at the same time. Limit the work you have in progress at any time.

The more work you have in progress, the longer it will take you to complete anything. This is risky because the longer it takes you to achieve things, the more likely you will lose motivation and give up. Completing work gives a feeling of satisfaction and achievement that is important to keep you going in the long run.

This is also an excellent reason to break big pieces of work into smaller units. You can keep yourself motivated by completing tasks and working towards more significant achievements. Smaller units of work are also easier to manage. Many of the most important achievements we seek will require substantial and sustained work over long periods, so staying motivated is essential.

Some things have real deadlines, and the more work you have in progress, the less likely you will be to complete the work in time. Complete the deadline-driven work and then move on to the other work when it is completed. Be sure the deadlines are real deadlines. An example of deadline-driven work is your personal tax return. This must be achieved and submitted by a date stated by your tax authority, and failure to do so may result in a penalty.

Working on many things simultaneously also dramatically increases the chance that your work will have reduced or no value after completing it. If you work on ten things simultaneously, it will take you 10x as long to deliver them than it would you had worked on one thing at a time as you will have to manage the extra work as well as do it and deal with the efficiency impact that context switching brings.

Working on one thing at a time lets you complete each task faster, giving you more benefit from the result. Big batches of work often feel more logical, but they delay the realisation of value and are not a good idea if your work is complex and subject to change.

On my website, TheScrumMaster.co.uk, I have a range of practice assessments which help people to prepare to sit the official assessments to gain certifications in Scrum from Scrum.org. At one point, I had a Goal to create eight new practice assessments. My instinct was to work on these in 1 batch and release them all together. I may gain some efficiencies working this way. However, creating them took significant time, and my forecast suggested it could take eight months to complete the work. This was a long time, and I was not happy waiting this long to deliver value to my customers.

Instead, I worked on each practice assessment independently and launched one each month. In the end, it still took me eight months to complete the work, but doing it this way brought two significant benefits.

Firstly, my clients could start using each practice assessment as soon as it launched rather than waiting up to 8 months. This helped over 1000 people that would have otherwise had to manage without them. Also, we charge a small amount for each practice assessment and donate all the profits to charity. By building the practice assessments individually and launching them as soon as they were done, we could donate profits to our charity of choice that would otherwise not have existed if we had worked on a single large batch.

To limit the amount of work I take on, I set a limit to how much work I will place into the Weekly Plan and Today Lists on my Kanban Board. Wherever possible, I work on one thing at a time and see it through to a conclusion before starting something else.

Anyone can start something; it is finishing work that is hard! It is persevering and seeing work through to its completion that moves you towards your Goals, so finishing is where your focus should be. It is almost always better to finish something you have already started rather than start something new. Small batches are desirable when the work is ever-changing, and you need to maintain motivation and progress towards your Goal.

Just In Time Decision Making

Life can be challenging. To move forward, make progress and be successful, we need to make crucial decisions on what to spend time on and what not to. Our time and other resources are limited. The information we have when we need to make these critical decisions is usually incomplete, yet at a certain point, we have to make choices which will affect the future direction of our lives. Making decisions is difficult.

Sometimes decisions need to be made immediately. The more minor day-to-day decisions with fewer consequences can be made and reversed if necessary. However, even making small decisions uses energy and can lead to decision fatigue. Decision fatigue is when the mind becomes fatigued after a sustained decision-making period. Making decisions is a cognitively taxing process, and decision-making ability declines after long decision-making periods. This is something to be aware of, and if it is something you experience, you should make changes to help eliminate the volume of decisions you need to make each day. This is why many people create routines and take comfort in them. They allow us to act on fewer decisions and save time and energy.

Steve Jobs wore a black turtleneck and jeans every day. Barack Obama wears only grey or blue suits. Albert Einstein had a closet full of the same grey suit. This was a conscious choice on their part to reduce the decisions they had to make each day to save time and energy for more important things.

Small strategies can help save small amounts of energy each day. It is the bigger decisions that take significant thought and energy. Should we change jobs? Should we start a business? Should we change careers? These are decisions that will have far-reaching consequences in our lives. In making them, we must deal with incomplete information and attempt to predict possible futures. These decisions are much more complicated and maybe even impossible to reverse, so the stakes are high.

A powerful strategy to help us make the best decisions when the stakes are high like this is Just-In-Time decision-making. This is the purposeful delay of decisions until the last responsible moment, the point where the cost of not making a decision exceeds the cost of making it, or when failure to make a decision, results in a decision being made by default.

When making significant complex decisions, we want to maximise the information at our disposal. Deciding as late as possible ensures we have the latest up-to-date information at our disposal, which increases the chance of a good or the right decision being made.

In the Personal Scrum System, these decisions can be added to the To Do List and parked for later. We have recorded the need for them, so they will not be forgotten. The planning events mean we will regularly revisit them and can move the decision into a Weekly Plan if the time has come to deal with it and make the decision. The energy saved can be used for other essential things.

Just-In-Time Decision-making is another superpower. Since I have started consciously doing this, I have made a far greater number of good decisions. Leaving the big decision until the time when you have the most information available leads to better decisions. Simple!

Traditional To Do Lists Do Not Work

For many years I used a basic To Do list to manage my Activities. Eventually, I realised they do not work for anything beyond the simple.

The things we need to do are not always one-dimensional and cannot be worked on one at a time before moving on to the next. At any given time, we will likely have several Activities underway. Some work will be on hold, waiting for feedback or an external contribution, some things cannot be started until a specific date, while others must be finished by a fixed date.

When I used a To Do list, I was constantly re-adjusting the order of items on the list, and it was impossible to plan and understand what should happen and when. The system didn't allow for the complexity of life and all the competing demands we face. A one-dimensional To Do List makes it incredibly difficult to see what is happening.

This is why the Personal Scrum System makes use of more than a single list with multidimensional views of Goals & Activities becoming possible. The Lists in your Kanban board allow a simple visualisation of all of this at various levels.

Personal Scrum separates Goals (where you want to get to), Measures (how you know you are getting there), Activities (what you need to do to reach your Goals) and Tasks (what you need to do to complete the Activities). These distinct groups provide a logical hierarchy that helps you understand how the low-level Tasks you carry out ultimately contribute to your Goals.

Get Help

Doing everything yourself is lonely, exhausting and a suboptimal way to work. Are you the best-placed person to do everything? Are there some things that bringing in an expert would help? Could some things of low value, but that need to be done nonetheless, be done by someone else? If the answer to any of these is yes, then you may want to get help.

When I started my training business, I made the mistake of trying to do everything myself. As a result, things took much longer than I had wished, and I ended up working long and unsustainable hours, which affected the quality of my work. Things rapidly improved when I decided to get help and bring people in to help me with certain activities.

Initially, I hired someone to take over customer support and handle any communications with our clients. This meant they got faster responses, and I saved a lot of time which I used to focus better on the training I provided and creating new products.

Bringing in help had some significant benefits:

- More focus on my Goals.
- More free time to rest, relax and recharge to maintain high-quality work.
- Reduced sources of distraction. Having someone else replying to the constant stream of messages and calls creates more focused time to do high-value work.

- Bringing in specialists to do things increases the quality of the work.

While you might not need to hire someone full-time, there are plenty of opportunities to find people to help you with certain Activities. You could:

- Hire a virtual assistant to take over many of your admin tasks
- Hire a specialist to carry out specific tasks for you. This could range from design to marketing to web development and more.
- Find partners who can help you to do certain things.

Say No!

"The World Doesn't Need Your Explanation. On Saying 'No': say, 'I can't do it. I hope everything is well." - James Altucher. Tools Of Titans[1].

It is very tough to get anything done if your default response to requests and queries is "yes." Saying yes to every request will send you in many different directions when you will likely only have the time, energy, and resources to go in one. Saying yes too often creates distractions that will keep you from focusing on the few things that matter.

Mastering the ability to say "no" is essential to being successful. Our resources are finite, and our progress will slow if we take on too much. While this can be challenging, as we don't want to miss out on an opportunity, we must make careful choices aligned with our current Goals.

Whilst it can be a good practice to briefly explain why you are rejecting a request, you should not feel that you must always do this. You don't owe the person a reason. Often saying no nicely but firmly is enough.

When I started my training business in the early years, I said yes to almost everything. I often ended up working 60-hour weeks and quickly became exhausted. I have since adjusted my default answer for requests for my time and efforts to be a "no". It's not that I do not want to help people, because I do. But I realised that I needed to focus my energies on the things I had already committed to and support the people I had agreed to help. If I took on too much, eventually, I would be unable to help anyone effectively, including myself.

I now turn down more requests than I accept. Typically, a ratio of 10 "noes" to every 1 "yes". Do I miss out on opportunities? Sometimes, but at least I make the most of the options I accept and protect myself from burnout.

Kaizen - Continuous Improvement

Kaizen[1] is the Japanese philosophy and practice of Continuous Improvement.

The concept was first implemented in the West to help improve manufacturing output in the USA during World War 2.

After World War 2, as part of their national rebuild programme, the Japanese took the successful concept of Continuous Improvement and adapted it and incorporated it into Kaizen. The new approach formed the foundation from which the Japanese built a thriving manufacturing industry.

Although Kaizen was developed to help businesses improve and thrive, it is just as applicable to our personal lives and can be used alongside the Personal Scrum System.

We can improve our lives by continuously learning, growing and improving. The philosophy of Kaizen is based on the concept that instead of making big changes at once, we focus on making small incremental improvements over a longer time. Make small improvements regularly that will gradually lead to the change you want.

As part of my Weekly Planning, I aim to include one process improvement to make something faster/better/easier for me in future. Doing so ensures I am continuously improving.

Here are some examples of recent process improvements that I carried out:

* * *

- Re-wrote the post-purchase message sent to customers who have purchased a course to make the information clearer.
- Automated a bookkeeping practice to save me a few minutes each time we run a course.
- Set up three email rules to prevent certain newsletters from appearing in my Inbox. Instead, I will check and review them every month.
- Activated increased automation on the comments moderation system on TheScrumMaster.co.uk so I do not need to check submitted comments manually.
- Activated a Spam protection app on my phone so more Spam phone calls will be blocked before reaching me.

While these changes may only save me a few minutes each day, those minutes add up and will prove significant over a longer time. The time I save can be used to do something valuable.

Don't fall into the trap of being a "busy fool" who gets stuck doing low-value work that doesn't help you towards your Goals. Use Kaizen/Continuous Improvement to make small incremental improvements so you are regularly getting better at what you do and how you do it.

Invest In Yourself

For many years, the only formal training I undertook for myself was provided by my employers. Some of them regularly invested in training me, while others did not. When I first became self-employed, I realised that no one else would pay for my training, which was now down to me.

I did not take any training for a few years as I was carefully managing my funds. I was still investing in other areas, but I had stopped investing in myself directly through training. I contributed to my pension and carefully saved any excess money I made, but any benefits from this would be far off in the future and would not help me know. I started to realise that I was failing to invest sufficiently in myself in the present and that this was a mistake.

If you take a training course which costs £1,000, but sometime later, the skills you develop help you secure a £10,000 pay rise, then you have received an almost immediate 10x return on your investment. This will further compound as you will receive that £10,000 extra every year you work until you eventually retire. Your return on investment could be hundreds of thousands of pounds in the long term. That is a fantastic return on your initial £1,000 and far more than you would get from a savings account, property or any other form of investment.

Investing in improving yourself, your skills, and your capabilities will substantially benefit you. The more skills and experience you develop, the more career choices you will have. Your confidence will increase as your abilities rise. You will experience higher satisfaction in your work as you become more able to offer value to your employer, clients, or colleagues.

Investing in yourself is not just about spending money on training. You can also invest in books, certifications, tools, and anything else that will help you to get better at what you do. You should also ensure you take sufficient rest, holidays, exercise and sleep to maintain your energy levels and prevent burnout. These things may cost you some money, but if that helps you to get better at what you do, it will be money well spent.

Mentors and Coaches

Finding someone to act as a Mentor or a Coach to help you improve is a great thing to do. It can help you achieve your Goals faster.

A Mentor is someone who can provide guidance, advice, support, motivation and act as a role model. They are typically someone with greater experience than you in your chosen field, and are willing to work with you to help guide you down the right path. The arrangement with a Mentor can be either formal or informal. An experienced Mentor to provide guidance and support can be a huge benefit, you can benefit from their wisdom and experience to progress faster in your chosen field.

An alternative to mentoring is to work with a Coach. An experienced Coach will help you to learn and develop without necessarily providing the context-specific advice that a Mentor may offer. A Coach can help you remove the biggest obstacles to success, which are often internal rather than external.

I have been lucky to benefit from the help of an experienced Coach over the years. My Coach helped me to build confidence, explore new options and realise that more things were possible than first seemed possible.

CHAPTER SIX

Getting Started

How To Start Using the Personal Scrum System

The Personal Scrum System is designed so you can learn about it and start using it within one hour.

This system will help you clarify your Goals and plan the Activities you will need to carry out to reach them. This will help increase the chance of you maintaining focus and making meaningful progress. While nothing can guarantee you will be successful, the Personal Scrum System will significantly increase the probability of this.

To help you get started quickly, you can make use of the following resources:

- Templates for the Lists you will need to use the Personal Scrum System, including example Goals & Activities.
- Resources to learn more about the Personal Scrum System.
- Tools & other resources mentioned throughout this book.

All of these can be found at:
https://www.thescrummaster.co.uk/PSS-resources

CHAPTER SEVEN
Appendix

Glossary

Personal Scrum System - A system to help you achieve success by defining Goals and Activities and then planning and managing progress towards them weekly, monthly and yearly. It helps you make your Goals, Activities, planning and progress transparent. It helps you ensure you are doing the right Activities to achieve the right Goals. It helps you maintain focus and motivation as you carry out the Activities to achieve your Goals.

<u>Lists - Make Goals & Activities transparent and manageable.</u>

- **Ideas List** - Goals & Activities that you are thinking about but have not yet committed to.
- **Goals List** - The Goals you have set and decided to work towards.
- **To Do List** - The Activities you have identified to help you achieve your Goals.
- **This Week List** - The Goals & Activities you have planned for this week.
- **Today List -** The Activities you plan to do today.
- **In Progress List** - The Activities you are actively doing.
- **On Hold List-** The Activities that are waiting on someone or something else.
- **Done List** - The Goals & Activities completed so far.

* * *

<u>Events - Allocated time to review progress and make plans.</u>

- **Weekly Planning** - Where you plan the Goals and forecast the Activities you will carry out during the next week.
- **Daily Planning** - Where you plan and forecast the Activities you will carry out during the next day.
- **Quarterly Planning** - Where you plan the Goals and Activities you aim to focus on in the next 3 months. New Goals & Activities may emerge. Existing plans may change.
- **Yearly Planning** - Where you plan the Goals and Activities you aim to focus on in the next year. New Goals & Activities may emerge. Existing plans may change.
- **Ongoing Planning** - The act of reviewing, updating and planning Goals, Activities & Tasks. This can occur at any time.

<u>Other Terminology - Other terms related to the Personal Scrum System</u>

- **Weekly Plan** - The Goals & Activities you have planned for the next week.
- **Goals -** Your aims, where you want to get to. Something you aspire to achieve.
- **Strategic Goal -** A long-term or "big picture" Goal
- **Intermediate Goals -** A short to medium term Goal that will move you towards a Strategic Goal.
- **Activities** - The Activities you will carry out to reach your Goals
- **Tasks** - A lower-level unit of Activity that you will carry out. One Activity may have many Tasks you will carry out to get it done.
- **Measures** - The things you will measure to understand if you are making progress towards a Goal

- **Kanban Board** - A tool to visualise your Lists to make them easier to view and manage.

Simon Kneafsey is the Principal Trainer at TheScrumMaster.co.uk and a Scrum.org Professional Scrum Trainer (PST).

He is on a mission to simplify Scrum & Agile for 1 million

people. He has helped 10,000+ people across 1000+ organisations so far, and he can help you too!

Simon comes highly recommended with 700+ personal LinkedIn recommendations. He is 5-star rated on Trustpilot & Google. His clients include Google, NASA, the United Nations, Toyota, Coca-Cola and many more.

Simon is based in London, UK and offers Scrum & Agile training courses online and in-person all over the world. You can reach him at TheScrumMaster.co.uk

What Did You Think of the Personal Scrum System?

First of all, thank you for purchasing this book. I know you could have picked any number of books to read, but you picked this book and for that I am extremely grateful.

If you enjoyed this book and found some value, I'd like to hear from you and hope that you will take some time to post a short review on Amazon. Your feedback and support will help me to improve my writing and make this book even better.

You can follow this link to leave a review on Amazon:
   https://www.thescrummaster.co.uk/PSS-AmazonReview

Finally, it would also be really nice if you could share this book with your friends and colleagues by posting a mention to LinkedIn, Facebook and/or Twitter.

Acknowledgements

Acknowledgements and thanks to the following people:

- Ken Schwaber & Jeff Sutherland, the co-creators of Scrum[1], on which the Personal Scrum System is based.
- David Anderson, originator of the Kanban Method.

Notes

Success != Happiness

[1]   What to Know About the Hedonic Treadmill and Your Happiness
https://www.healthline.com/health/hedonic-treadmill

What If I Don't Know What My Goal Should Be?

[1]   The 7 Habits of Highly Effective People
https://www.amazon.co.uk/Habits-Highly-Effective-People-
Infographics-ebook/dp/B09LZ766JN/ref=tmm_kin_swatch_0?
_encoding=UTF8&qid=1661857117&sr=8-3

[2]   The First and Second Laws of Motion
https://www.grc.nasa.gov/www/k-12/WindTunnel/Activities/
first2nd_lawsf_motion.html#:~:text=Newton's%20First%20Law%2
0of%20Motion,upon%20by%20an%20outside%20force

The Power Of Having Clear Goals

[1]   Could 'After Earth' End Will Smith's Box Office Domination?
https://www.hollywoodreporter.com/news/general-news/after-
earth-end-will-smiths-561647/

Measuring Progress

[1]   Measurement Myopia
https://www.drucker.institute/thedx/measurement-myopia/

Done List

[1]   Twitter Tweet
https://twitter.com/ChuckDurfee/status/307192324096675840

* * *

Learning

[1]   17 Remarkable Career Change Statistics To Know (2022)
https://www.apollotechnical.com/career-change-statistics/

Flow State

[1]   The Concept of Flow
https://link.springer.com/chapter/10.1007/978-94-017-9088-8_16

Timeboxing

[1]   Parkinson's Law
https://www.economist.com/news/1955/11/19/parkinsons-law

The 80/20 Rule

[1]   Pareto Principle
https://en.wikipedia.org/wiki/Pareto_principle
[2]   The 80/20 Rule And How It Can Change Your Life
https://www.forbes.com/sites/kevinkruse/2016/03/07/80-20-rule/?sh=7a2609a93814
[3]   United Nations Development Program (1992), 1992 Human Development Report, New York: Oxford University Press
[4]   Rooney, Paula (October 3, 2002), Microsoft's CEO: 80–20 Rule Applies To Bugs, Not Just Features, ChannelWeb
https://www.crn.com/news/security/18821726/microsofts-ceo-80-20-rule-applies-to-bugs-not-just-features.htm
[5]   Weinberg, Myrl (July 27, 2009). "Myrl Weinberg: In health-care reform, the 20-80 solution". The Providence Journal. Archived from the original on 2009-08-02.
https://web.archive.org/web/20090802002952/http://www.projo.com/opinion/contributors/content/CT_weinberg27_07-27-09_HQF0P1E_v15.3f89889.html

SMART Goals

[1]   SMART Goals
https://corporatefinanceinstitute.com/resources/knowledge/other/smart-goal

* * *

Say No!

[1] Tools of Titans
https://www.amazon.co.uk/Tools-Titans-Billionaires-World-Class-Performers-ebook/dp/B01LF32ZNU/ref=tmm_kin_swatch_0?_encoding=UTF8&qid=1661857883&sr=8-1

Kaizen - Continuous Improvement

[1] MindTools: Kaizen: Gaining the Full Benefits of Continuous Improvement
https://www.mindtools.com/pages/article/newSTR_97.htm

Acknowledgements

[1] This book is neither endorsed by nor affiliated with Scrum.org. This document uses content (adapted) from the Scrum Guide. All the content related to Scrum Guide is taken from scrumguides.org and is under the Attribution ShareAlike license of Creative Commons. Further information is accessible at
http://creativecommons.org/licenses/by-sa/4.0/legalcode
and also described in summary form at
http://creativecommons.org/licenses/by-sa/4.0